bash

b a s h
latterday plays

neil labute

the overlook press
woodstock • new york

First published in the United States in 1999 by
The Overlook Press, Peter Mayer Publishers, Inc.
Lewis Hollow Road
Woodstock, New York 12498

Cataloging-in-Publication data is available
from the Library of Congress

Book design and type formatting by Bernard Schleifer

Manufactured in the United States of America
First Edition

1 3 5 7 9 8 6 4 2

ISBN 1-58567-024-3

for emma, chet, and billie

bash premiered in new york city
at the douglas fairbanks theater
on june 24, 1999.
the cast was as follows:

iphigenia in orem
young man ....ron eldard

a gaggle of saints
john ....paul rudd
sue..............calista flockhart

medea redux
woman ......calista flockhart

produced by eric krebs and stephen pevner
directed by joe mantello
scenic design by scott pask
costume design by lynette meyer
lighting design by james vermuelen
sound design by red ramona

contents

iphigenia in orem

silence. darkness.

**lights up slowly to reveal
a young man, early 30s,
dressed in a plain suit.
he is seated on the edge of
a hotel chair and nurses a
water glass in one hand.**

YOUNG MAN

...i'll tell it once. one time because it deserves to be
told, and then never again. fair enough? well,
doesn't really matter what you think. i mean, i
care, i do, i want you to listen to this, hear me out,
but it's not really important how you feel about it
all in the end...it's happened now. and i don't
know you from adam...or eve, for that matter.
(LAUGHS) sorry, i'm just trying to keep this...
yeah, anyway. your drink okay? there's plenty over
on the counter there, so feel free...the looser the
better on this one, i figure, so bottoms up, or
whatever they say at the bar these days. i wouldn't
know. really, feel free...comes with the room.

(BEAT) i'm not a drinker...you probably guessed
that, though, right? yeah...nothing but water here.
(HOLDS UP GLASS) never was, but when i saw
you down in the lounge i could tell right away that
you enjoyed the stuff. what is that you've got
there? some kind of red, what, wine, is it? looks
like it. wine. do, really, feel at home. all that's just
gonna go to waste if you don't...well, the next
person'll drink it maybe, but you know what i
mean. myself, i hate to waste things... (BEAT) so anyway, when i spotted you, alone like you were and
going through that bottle, i figured you'd be a
great listener. that you wouldn't mind if i told you
all this... and if i'm lucky, by tomorrow, you won't
even remember it. i'm kidding, but you're okay,
comfortable? good. (BEAT) so...where should i...let
me see. alright. i never used to travel. pretty much
stayed in our branch office, did things over the
phone, handled it all that way. you know? never
cared much for driving all the time, meeting
clients, that end of things...i mean, i did it when i
first started, low man on the pole and whatever,
but once i got the old m.b.a., foot in the door and
all...i stuck to the desk as much as i could. i like it.
that office...i don't know..."feel." the atmosphere.
faxes coming in, people zipping around, emer-
gency strategy sessions, all that. it's like being a kid
again, playing at "war" or that type of thing. i
don't mean exactly like that, but you know what
i'm saying. it's a whole different thing out there, i

have to tell you. the world of business. it is. all that
"dog eat dog," "jungle out there" stuff has become
pretty cliché now, but it's true. i mean, you can see
what guys love about it. and i don't mean just guys
either, because there's plenty of women in the
field, too, obviously, but i mean "guys" like in...
well, "guys." you know, how it's used these days.
all encompassing. it's very high stakes, lots of cash
floating around you, and the pressure's a real...
well, just hot. day in and out. seriously. it is. we
may play it like a game sometimes, but believe me,
a day doesn't go by in business that you're not out
for somebody's blood...
pause.
but, hey, you know what i'm talking about...you're
in what, sales? yeah, i thought so. you look like...
well, no, i mean it in a complimentary...you just
look like you could sell. things. if you wanted to...
pause.
i guess the point i'm making is that it's a stress-
filled situation i'm in, but i'm paid for it, not com-
plaining. i just wanted to, i don't know, lead in the
right way on this. i'm not making excuses. i'm
not... (BEAT) okay, so, once i got the degree, i
went to the "y" for it, they've got a pretty decent
program and it's important, i think anyhow, to get
your schooling from different places and since we
lived in salt lake i'd gone to the "u" for my under-
graduate...'cause the whole b.y.u. thing sounded a
little intense for me when i was eighteen...not that

i was, i don't know, like a rebel or anything, far
from it, but i'd decided in high school not to go
the mission route until after i had finished college.
maybe when i was married or something...i wanted
to get right out there in the job market as quick
as i could. looks like i'm losing you. i'm l.d.s., you
know, "mormon?" yeah. see, a "mission" is where
you go...oh, okay, so you know what i'm talking
about. good. i figured you did, i mean, las vegas
isn't that far from...must be getting late. i'll try and
be...brief—things took a bit of a turn for us last
year. well, i guess about a year and a half ago, now.
my wife and me, the family, you know...we lost a
child. newborn. well, five months old...just like
that. just happened. (BEAT) i was off that day, a
friday, i think, and deborah, that's my wife, deb,
she was out—her mother was staying with us, and
they were over at safeway getting some milk—deb
put the baby down, "emma" we'd named her, she
put emma in our bed because that's where she'd
been sleeping the first few months...we always
thought that was a good bonding thing, i'd read it
somewhere, or she heard it at relief society or
something like that...anyway, so that's what she
did. she tucks her in, and out they went. and see, i
was gonna lie down with her, i really was, but i just
went back into the living room for a second, watch
a little *wheel of fortune* or some thing, you know,
five minutes a week to myself. and i fell. fell off to
sleep right there, there on the loveseat by the win-

dow. (BEAT) deb's mom...emma's grandma...
found her. maybe a half hour later. she'd smoth-
ered herself under the covers, i don't know,
beneath the weight of the comforter or whatever it
was. this big old maroon and gold thing we'd gotten as a wedding gift, huge—and she'd, well, she'd
suffocated. that's about as plain as you can tell it,
right? the little thing...died in our bed, tangling
herself in the blankets. (BEAT) the police had to
come, they do for any kind of infant death, that's
what the officer said; i'd gotten a hold of myself by
that time, still crying, but deb...deb was just kind
of sitting there next to me, staring off, and this
guy—this person—a detective, i suppose, was ask-
ing us questions. standing there and firing off this
series of questions. "standard procedure," he
assured us, but still...

pause.

what bothered him...no, "puzzled" him, he said,
never came right out and said it bothered him but
you could see by the way he...he didn't understand
how the baby could get so far down. (BEAT) now i
am losing you, right? okay, yeah, i'm getting ahead
of myself...it seemed to him that the baby, a baby
that young and small, she was such a small little
thing...was too far down toward the foot of the
bed, and turned. something about that seemed to
be eating at him. i didn't understand what he was
getting at, the way he kept going back and forth
over the events and times and all that, "where were
you standing?" and "approximately how long were

you...?" blah, blah, blah. i mean, my god, we're sitting there on the edge of the sofa, the bed my daughter has just died in i can see through an open door back down the hallway, and this man is pacing around, sucking on the chewed cap of a ballpoint pen and...asking me quietly, "did you check on her?" (BEAT) what's he getting at, anyway? i mean, that's a no-win, isn't it? think about it...if i didn't check on her, i'm not a good father, not anything he can say about it, but i carry around the guilt, you know...maybe i could've prevented it. right? and if i did go in there, if i had've done what i was supposed to do, had planned on doing, the nap...then maybe she'd be alive. maybe. (BEAT) and for just a second, just the briefest of moments...i catch deb looking over at me. as if this is the first time the thought's come to her as well. this possibility. the whole incident hangs there— probably only two or three seconds all together— but it just lays there in the air over us all. this shadow of a doubt...there's another cliché for you...it hangs there until i say, very matter-of-factly, "umm, no, i didn't. i meant to, but..." and off he goes. says "fine," stops me cold, and off he goes. onto another tangent... (BEAT) she took my hand in hers, deb did, just after that. scooped it up into her tiny fingers and held it there...all the rest of that afternoon. even after the police were gone, as we sat there into the evening with her mother, our two other children, home from school and having

heard it all...none of us talking, just sitting and
watching the darkness crowd into the room...she
held onto my hand. and somehow, because of that,
i felt at peace... (BEAT) anyway, the detective said
that he was nearly done, just one or two more
items, when deborah grabbed hold of my hand
like she did. when she did that...
pause.
all during this i can see guys passing—oops, i
mean "people"—i can see these people passing in
front of the doorway. i could, deb was just off to
the side enough to miss it, thank heavens...
tweezers all out, picking up scraps of whatever, the
snap! of flashbulbs, some muffled talk about an
upcoming jazz game...i'm starting to feel queasy.
the heat of the room, maybe, and the sitting there
as this almost unbearable thing unfolds in front of
us...we'd hardly had a moment to hold each other,
deborah and myself, to cry and, you know, just...
and this happens. this *dragnet* episode takes place
right in our living room...and i start to feel sick. i
did. i hide it pretty well, but i felt it all the same...
pause.
and finally they were gone. i looked around, and
the front door slammed shut and it was empty. the
house. they'd taken emma out with them, the
coroner, maybe a half hour before, wrapped in a
little zip-up bag, something like what i carry my
pressed shirts in when i travel. i mean, i know i
said i don't like to go out on the road, i didn't

used to, anyway, but...well, just let me finish.
emma was gone, and we ate dinner...we may have
even ordered out that night; that probably sounds
horrible, but deborah just couldn't stand over the
stove right then, so it seems like we had a pizza...
yeah, one from sbarro's, over at the mall. we had
pizza, deb holding my hand under the table the
whole time, all through the silence...and we went
to bed right after. (BEAT) the phone woke me
about 11:30. i almost had to pry deborah's fingers
off of mine to get it, but i was on by about the
third, maybe the fourth ring. it was him. the police
detective and very apologetic about calling so late,
and the whole process and the usual stuff that
you'd see on any of those cop programs on tv. we
don't watch them much—maybe the kids do, when
we're not around, but they're not supposed to—
but you know the kind i mean. he was like that...
(BEAT) it'd all come out fine, he said, ruled
"natural causes" after a few tests'd been run and he
just wanted to let us know and if there was anything he could do he'd be glad to...i hung up without him finishing. he'd put us through enough
that day. on a day like that, a day no parent should
ever have to face, and to have those...people do
that...so i hung up. i hung up the receiver and
rolled back over to deborah. i just held her at first...
putting my hand back in place and squeezing her
fingers a bit. but it woke her. she woke up and we
whispered to each other...talking under the sheets

like two schoolchildren, about things we hadn't
mentioned in years! we were under the sheets, just
them, because from that night on, deb and i could
never sleep with blankets on that bed again...that's
probably odd, isn't it? maybe not...but we couldn't.
middle of winter, kids'll all be off at ski trips up at
aspen grove or sundance and deborah and me just
huddle together under the sheets. to this day...
(BEAT) anyhow, the talking must've gone on for
hours, a few at least and then the kissing and finally
...well, you're not that drunk. you don't need to
hear it all. we did what you'd imagine you might
do on a night like that, a moment when your
entire universe has been changed forever. (BEAT)
i don't know, but that may have even been the
night that joe was...that's our youngest, "joseph,"
yes, named after our prophet, and i have a brother
of the same name, so...but joe came almost exactly
nine months later. he's a great boy, he really is.
and over time, and with the new child...life goes
on. it does, and it's strange to say that, you know,
because i'd never believe it from hearing some
other person say it, i mean, like at fast and testi-
mony. if i heard that i'd just never buy it, because
of the loss, and you know, i'd feel everybody was
just smiling and pretending to be all understanding,
but they really think that you're like some chinese
family getting rid of the daughter to get a son
and just crazy things'd run through my head...
but then it happens to you, and it's true. (BEAT)

you just go on. you do. you thank your heavenly
father for giving you strength to stand up to his
trials and figure there must be a plan behind it all,
a reason for so much pain and you just...go on.
pause.
and that's what we did. we went on...and more
than that. a lot more... (BEAT) lemme fill your
glass there or you're not gonna...well, okay. if
you're fine, then you're fine. umm... (BEAT)
so...so, so, so.
pause.
i've gotten off the path here...somehow. (CHECKS
WATCH) umm, look at the...you're sure you've
got the time for this? (BEAT) well, there's not
much left to tell, anyhow, so finish off that drink
and i'll be done...i promise.
pause.
alright. umm...there was a problem. that's what
had started all this, i mean, originally. started it all
in motion...a problem at work. we'd been taken
over recently, i mean, no big deal in theory, happened all the time during the 80s, somebody else
takes over, you lose a few of the stragglers, guys
who couldn't keep up...and i do mean "guys" as in
everybody, all people here, because it was usually
women at that point. not always, but a lot of the
time...takeovers were an excellent way to get
things back in order. and that's not just me
talking, you know...there's definitely an order to
things in business, and the old boys at the top, the

guys you never even see, just their pictures in the
hallway...they like things the way they've always
been. so that's when a bunch of these women with
their m.b.a.s and affirmative action nonsense
would get the boot. nothing personal about it, at
least i never felt there was...just getting everything
spinning back the way it was supposed to be.
(BEAT) but not this time. no, this time it was
gonna happen, and nobody could tell which way
things would end up. everybody at my level, that
mid-management level of things...was pretty
vulnerable and it came down that we could count on
four of us from the salt lake office—that's where i
worked, commuted in from orem every day
because of the standard of living that area afforded
us—and it'd just be up to fate as to who got the
axe. another cliché, right? yeah, well, i'm full of
'em. or it, full of it, one of the two...can't be sure
anymore. (BEAT) so, that was the story, four of us
were going to go, three of which i and everyone
else had a pretty good idea of, three that should've
gone a long time ago, but that last spot...that was
the one. the tough call. there was me, who'd been
steady and strong and average, you know, just
average or slightly above, someone that they could
count on, good sense of humor and everything for
the past seven years. well liked and i liked everyone. or, most everyone. there was this woman, a
few years younger than me and had come in during
a wave of new hires about four years back...just

plain vicious. i mean, talk about clichés and all
that, she was a walking one...the business suit and
blunt cut hair thing going, can't remember ever
even seeing her smile, you know what i'm saying...
but she knew her stuff. i knew it, we all did, and
so did she and she reveled in it. the sales, the
numbers, the whole game. we'd gotten off badly
...actually, i'd made a mistake once, a board meeting
where i'd grouped her in with a "you guys oughta..."
meaning that side of the table and she called me
out on it...first meeting, or maybe the second,
she'd been to and she nails me out loud about my
attitude, my limited "chauvinist lexicon" and all this
other, just, crap that she fired off. walked out of
the room in silence and me and some of the other
guys laughed it off over lunch, but i caught one or
two of the other women smiling to themselves as
the meeting broke up. just this slight thing, but i
caught it...anyway, i always felt one step behind
her after that, like she made it her job to one up
me from that moment on... (BEAT) but she was
one. me, and her, because of the short time she'd
been there, and a couple other folks that had
about the same seniority that i did...and that's
what hung over our heads, each of us, day after
day as we'd go into work. it was coming, we knew
that, it was going to happen and all we could do
was look at each other as we sat there waiting...
pause.

i got the call just before deb had gone to safeway.
took it in the den because it was coming from
chicago...a friend of mine, at the home office, a
guy from school actually, with a tip. a tip he'd
heard that day and wanted to call me with it...it
was me. i was the one that would make up the
four, and he was so sorry and all that—he's a really
good guy, i see him whenever i'm in chicago, we
were these really big jokers when we were at the
"u," in the dorms together and so he was just
doing what any guy would do, he said, letting me
hear it from a friendly voice, and giving me a
jump, the weekend, anyway. before he hung up he
said again it was just what was going around, but
he thought i should know... (BEAT) i couldn't even
look at deb as she was going out to the van. she
called out to me, told me to crawl in and get a little
snooze before the kids got home and they'd be
right back...but i just waved to her. couldn't look,
you know, not right then, just waved my hand, i
was too busy looking around the house, at our
things. i mean, all the things we'd gathered in ten
years together, and at the house itself and, well,
just all of it...what was i gonna do? how could i
possibly keep it all going, the lifestyle we'd made
for ourselves, without my seniority, the benefit
package...jobs all over being tight like they are? it
just wouldn't be possible... (BEAT) it was like the
moment in that film *kramer vs. kramer*, you know,
where he decides he's got to get a job that day,

right? i felt like that...i keep bringing up movies
and tv and i don't mean to, because we really don't
watch all that much, but there is some good pro-
gramming out there, and that was an especially
moving one, i thought, the way he fought that battle
with his wife over the child and...but i'm standing
there, just taking in the vcr, and our big screen tv
and one of the kid's bikes, i can see through the
front window, the pathfinder, *wheel of fortune*'s
blasting on the t v. in the family room...all these
thoughts are swirling around in my head. and i
hear it. (BEAT) i wasn't asleep...i couldn't of been,
i mean, i've tried to believe it, make myself believe
it, too, but i wasn't, or i never would've heard her.
the baby, emma, in the other room. as i was standing
there i heard her cry out from inside the bedroom. i did... (BEAT) when i got to the doorway
she was already under the blankets, she was, i
swear, under them and fighting to get out. it's just
reflexes, i guess, because she wasn't big enough to
do anything about it, i mean, she'd just started to
crawl a few weeks before that, and she was tiny for
her age, the doctors said that...but she'd managed
to get herself down under that comforter. i rushed
in there, to the edge of the carpet at the bedroom
door and then, i don't know, something stopped
me. just stopped me like some invisible force had
reached out and took hold of the back of my shirt
and yanked me to a halt...i looked in at her again,
this little yelp kind of coming up from her as she

blundered around in there...it almost looked like when your puppy, as a kid, or the family cat, you know, would get put under the blankets for a laugh, it was like that. almost. this little...mound... wandering around in there. it was nearly absurd, to walk in on something like this, i mean, you just could never be ready for a thing like that, and because of that, that specific part of it, the unreality ...i was able to make the decision. in that moment, standing there watching my daughter fight for her life, i made my decision. this is very hard to...any-way, remember i said i hated to waste things? well, when i looked at it, i mean, rationally, for even half-a-second there in the hallway, i realized that's what this was. an opportunity. and i wasn't going to waste it... (BEAT) so i—i'm just gonna say this, because it's a little...so. i went into the room and stood there by the bed, i stood there and pulled up the comforter by one corner and i saw her then. her little fine sandy hair and her...i just kind of coaxed her down a bit. down a bit further with the edge of my foot, turned her a touch and down and then i dropped the covers back and walked out...there was one last little sound emma made, you could barely hear it. but i just kept walking, back out to the loveseat, there in the family room, and layed down and made myself go to sleep. put a pillow over my head so i couldn't hear...and drifted off. (BEAT) the point i wanna make, though, see, is that it didn't have to happen that

way. i took the risk, this calculated risk for my family
that this whole episode would play out in our
favor, give me that little edge at work and maybe
things'd be okay, or they'd change their minds
because of, you know...but it didn't have to be like
that. if deb had just hurried a bit, if she hadn't
stop to look through *people* magazine or her mother
hadn't gone next door to fill a prescription, then
who knows? maybe they would've got back in time
and emma would still be...that sounds strange,
doesn't it, that way of thinking? but all i'm saying
is, it was fate that took her, just the whimsy of a
lingering red light or a prolonged chat with one
of our neighbors in the produce aisle or if i hadn't
heard her cry out in the first place. i mean, i
could've gotten into bed there beside her, i was
planning to, i might've fallen asleep and never
even heard her. then...who knows? it probably
would've happened anyway. and it did happen,
and so you go on. like i said before, you just go
on...
pause.
i kept my job. i did. and guess who was the one, i
mean, after all that, guess who got it right between
the eyes? another cliché, i know, but boy oh boy,
what a great one it was... (BEAT) i even walked
her to the elevator the day she left, her and the
other three, this was several months after all the
other...i was right behind them with a "so long"
and "we'll miss you" and right then, it came to me,
it came to me with my friends standing around

and that little...well, she wasn't looking so strong
anymore, there in the open car, this box of stuff in
her hands. as the doors were closing i said to them
all, but staring straight at her, i said, "you guys
take care now!" just like that, and then they slid
shut. huh...just like in *kramer* at the end. the doors
did...(GESTURES) isn't that funny? i never thought
of that before...i said that and we laughed all
through lunch about it, the guys and me.
pause.
i was at a seminar, big yearly thing the company
put on. this one was in boston, six months back.
my friend from chicago flew in for it. okay, so...
after the morning session, just in passing as we
were both in the restroom at one point, he said
something to me, my friend, i guess trying to
lighten things up a little, he mentioned work. and
about the layoffs, and how glad i must've finally
been to have gotten rid of you know who. and
then he said, "boy, i really had you going that
friday, didn't i?" i turned to him, standing there
at the urinal, my fly still open and i turned to him
and the whole picture was clear to me. right then,
it was as clear as a look into the future...what he'd
done. what we always used to do to each other. see,
he'd heard the real truth about what was coming
and just couldn't let it go without a little razzing
and so he'd given me the call, let me stew about it
over that weekend...he was going to buzz me back
monday morning with the truth. but by then...

(BEAT) yeah, he'd gotten me, alright. he got me
good, just like the old days.
pause.
so i travel now, same pay and everything, a little
better actually, but i consult for our regional
branches, even nationally sometimes...and it keeps
me going. deb and i are fine. joe's getting huge,
he really is, i'd show you a picture but i don't have
any on me...but i find i really like the driving these
days, you know? gives me a lot of time to just...
well, drive. just drive and think. i usually don't
even get a room; i got this place (GESTURES)
because i'm here a few days but normally, i'd have
everything in the trunk and just do it that way
...it's funny how things end up, isn't it? (BEAT)
i can't tell deb, it'd kill her. kill us, as a family, i
mean, that's obvious, right? can't tell anyone in the
church, or the police, of course...so i chose you. i
saw you, tonight as i was walking through the
lobby, and i just chose you. so there it is...i'm
finished.
pause.
you probably need to...yeah, it's late. take care of
yourself, and thanks again, seriously. you've been
very...you have any kids? no? well, when you do,
you be good to them, okay? there's nothing like
'em in the world...believe me. (BEAT) why don't
you go ahead and shut the light off there on your
way out, if you would...i'm just gonna sit here a

bit. i'll be fine. you go ahead, really, it's almost time for the last call, so you should...i'll be...fine, i will. (AFTER A MOMENT) goodnight...

> **he smiles weakly once and takes a last sip from his glass as the lights snap off.**
>
> **silence. darkness.**

a gaggle of saints

silence. darkness.

a young, attractive couple sitting apart from one another. they are dressed in the popular evening fashion of the day.

JOHN

so, okay, so there was this big bash...

SUE

a party...

JOHN

party, bash, whatever, in the city. that's what we came down for. the thing. this get-together. 's why we did it in the first place...

SUE

's our old ward, 2nd ward. i got a flyer in the mail...

JOHN

couple wards together, i think, mixed, and meeting in the city. ballroom over at the plaza...

SUE

which really sounded nice, you know...

JOHN

's expensive.

SUE

i mean, elegant.....

JOHN

but that's cool, manhattan, always have a good
time there, right?

SUE

people from high school were going...

JOHN

'cause we're juniors up at b.c., so, like, there's still
lots of guys we know...

SUE

seniors now, mostly...

JOHN

all these seniors, guys like that, who we're still in

touch with. friends, you know...

SUE

this was just after mid-terms...

JOHN

sue's a year ahead. almost. two semesters. we're
juniors, but nearly a year... (BEAT) both going to
b.c....

SUE

boston college. you know, we almost didn't get in. i
mean, both of us...

JOHN

my g.p.a. but we'd decided, i mean, early—like
back at greeley, junior year, maybe—that we'd do
college together.

SUE

and boston seemed about right, you know, four
hours from home...

JOHN

's a little over three, if you push it. i don't like to
go crazy with my vw, but it's only about three
hours if you're really moving. three, three and a
half...

SUE

it's beautiful up around there. i mean, massachusetts.
new england. all that's just gorgeous this time of
year. leaves turning...

JOHN

it just sounded really great, weekend back in new
york. stop in, maybe, say "hi" to the folks...be good
to go down for a couple days.

SUE

so i contacted the three people going to school
with us...you know, from our stake. three members
going to b.c. as well...

JOHN

one guy's even in my house, david's his name
...didn't really hang out with him at home or anything, different ward. and plays lacrosse, but he's
cool...

SUE

he's nice. nice guy...

JOHN

ended up, we talked two other couples into going
back with us...guy from the house, this david guy.

SUE

we took his car down...

JOHN

...and a friend of mine, tim, elder freeman, whatever...from my ward. year behind me, but studying
at b.c., same time...

SUE

's a beautiful red truck he had.
pause.
jeep or something...

JOHN

'cause i've got this old v.w., i said that, right? it's
great, '73, with the metal bumpers and all that
...but needs a tune-up and i'm not gonna drive
three hours with all these guys...

SUE

we all thought we could go down together. one
car. everybody wanted to, gonna be in the city at
this hotel, live band and everything...

JOHN

and so six of us, a girl that's going out with this
david from my fraternity, karen's her name, i
think...she was coming too. 's a non-member, but
coming 'cause she knew the city pretty well, grew
up just off the park and they were getting along
good...so it's six altogether now, six for the ride
and the v-dub's definitely out of the question.

SUE

david said he'd drive if we wanted.

JOHN

's got one of those isuzu troopers. 's roomy. big.

SUE

and we're all picked up at three in the afternoon, saturday.

JOHN

same weekend as preference up at school...but we hadn't planned on going, you know, so then sue gets the flyer and suddenly, i'm rushing around, fighting for tuxedos, ten minutes to six, friday afternoon! (BEAT) i ended up with a perry ellis. finally. a size big, but i got one...looks okay, doesn't it?

SUE

it looked good on him...i had to put a safety pin in the vest, in the back of it, but it was really nice when he had it on...

JOHN

we left 'em in the bags, the three of us guys, hanging in the trooper for the ride. i mean, no sense getting 'em messed up for no reason, right?

SUE

i had this dress i'd been saving...all taffeta. i'd been
saving it for something like this...did i mention
that? (BEAT) i needed to find some shoes, but i
thought the dress was perfect...

JOHN

we missed the game, b.c.'s first conference—'s
away, but we could've watched it at our place with
a bunch of guys, they always order in pizza and
everything—but we said "no," jump in with all
these people...road trip.

SUE

tim's girlfriend, patrice, i've known for years...

JOHN

with about a dozen overnight bags, tuxedos hanging from all corners of dave's isuzu... (BEAT) the
girls decided to wear their outfits...

SUE

it was my black dress.

JOHN

sue's got this knockout thing, kind of a cutaway in
the front, what's it called?

SUE

...with a scalloped neckline...

JOHN

"scalloped," i think...in the front, you know, over her chest and no back to it at all, not any sleeves, just very little on top. but chic, too, right? classic lines. see, it's a dinner dress, dress you'd wear out to dinner. dining. not something a girl would pick out, junior prom, with spaghetti straps all clotting it up... (BEAT) she looked great. proud to be with her...

SUE

i knew it'd get wrinkled, a little...i did. taffeta's terrible for that, but i thought it sounded wonderful, you know, getting out at some amoco, middle of connecticut, in this wave of taffeta...and buying, i don't know, a milky way, a can of soda. and the attendant's mouth just hanging open at the sight of us...

JOHN

i'm putting gas in, one time we stopped, and look up...i see nothing but chiffon and silk and whatnot, miles of it, going down the snack aisle. that killed me!...

SUE

i was carrying my shoes—i did find a pair, even had time to dye them to match—but i took 'em off in the car, and i was just holding them in the store. so, i'm standing there, in my stockings, carrying these shoes...

JOHN

i'll always remember that. her smiling at me,
through the glass there. little bit of chocolate on
her lips...and carrying her shoes.

SUE

this was going to be a great party...
pause
...i could feel it.

JOHN

the ward usually threw a pretty good bash, i mean,
times we'd go into the city...had my farewell there.
went to great britain.

SUE

it was our anniversary...

JOHN

last minute, got her a corsage. not the wrist kind,
hate those...but this was beautiful. white blossoms.
don't know what kind, but they were white. i
remember that...

SUE

i loved it! the softest pink, it was...john thought it
was white, but it was really just the lightest shade
of pink. the last shade of pink it could be, before
turning into something else... (BEAT) and you
know? he pricked his finger, john did. as he

pinned it on me, pricked his index finger...

JOHN

stupid pin!...

SUE

and then...a spot of blood, just a drop, but he ended up with this touch of blood on his shirt...

JOHN

couldn't even see it if i buttoned the jacket...

SUE

but see, in a weird way, though, it excited me. the blood. is that stupid to say?...probably, but it did. (BEAT) i mean, it was stunning to look at, you know? all that white on him, the bright of his shirt...and then this splash of...

JOHN

this red...

SUE

...blood on his chest.

JOHN

didn't get any on her dress, however. nothing. felt good about that...wouldn't want to ruin her anniversary dress.

SUE

six years...

JOHN

huh? believe that? six...since summer of our third
year in high school. wow...

SUE

i saw him on the track one day. lived six blocks
away all my life, in seminary together, but i never
really saw him until he was jogging one time...

JOHN

i like to keep in shape...

SUE

he'd always kept his hair short, trimmed up...

JOHN

my dad cut it. believe that?! sixteen years old and
my father drags me into the kitchen, every other
sunday—he was bishop at the time. i asked him if
this wasn't considered work, haircutting, but he
just said i had a big mouth—anyway, i could just
count on the standard "sears portrait" cut. (BEAT)
i was always a little worried about my ears. stick
out a bit...

SUE

but i see him running, really running, blistering by

people who are just jogging or walking and i don't
know this guy. 's cute. nice body. and i don't know
him... (BEAT) kind of long hair...

JOHN

my dad was away for the summer...teaching a sur-
vey course in lit over in london or some type of
thing...i didn't really know or care. i could let my
hair grow, that's what i saw coming out of the
whole deal. my mom didn't mind at all...

SUE

so i put down my softball glove, and my purse and
all that, and i start running, too. i mean, i can't
keep up with him but i go a little slower or a little
faster every so often so that he's catching me more
quickly on every lap.

JOHN

i knew who she was. she was dating a guy i knew...

SUE

that was over. we broke up, like, two weeks before.
he was this, i don't know, he'd kind of left the
church, and there's this completely bad scene at a
party. the screaming. and he's sort 'a drunk. and
so it's over. i mean, we're still calling each other
but it's definitely over...

JOHN

i'd heard this. i mean, you hear everything at
some time in your life, right, and this was a thing
you keep up on in high school. girls you secretly
like but can't get at 'cause they're dating somebody, maybe a friend, and so you file 'em away
and hope the guy joins the army or gets a mission
call to laos or something...held back in school,
even, and you and she end up on the same floor,
some dorm in florida. (BEAT) the best would be,
like, a major football moment, touchdown to take
the state championship, something majestic like
that, but anything...camp counselors even, would
do. she was that kind of girl...

SUE

and we're running together now, he's pretending
he's winded and needs to slow down and i'm just
trying to keep up and around we go. sun going
down, we're not speaking at all, and we just keep
going in circles...

JOHN

then he shows up...

SUE

we really had stopped dating. but he was going to
give me a ride home, just friendly, because the
track and the softball fields and everything are,
like, three miles from my house...

JOHN

he pulls his car right on the track. into the lanes.
nice new scirroco, all black, that he got as a gradu-
ation gift from his dad. he was a year or so older...

SUE

i slowed down a little.

JOHN

and i can see what's coming because i know him
and we've had some laughs together. not friends,
exactly, but friends of friends, that's what we are...

SUE

but i don't want to leave.

JOHN

this is how we first got together. it's kind of a
funny story...

SUE

so he chases me down on the track, because we
just jog by him, right around his car for a couple
laps, and keep going...

JOHN

why am i gonna stop? he's not my boyfriend...

SUE

we weren't really dating. you couldn't call it that,
anymore...

JOHN

see, and he grabs me. turns me around, after grabbing me, he turns me and says, "hey!" and he's
holding onto me, about my size, and one of his nails
is digging into my nipple, holding my chest like he
is. he's got these, like, long nails on one hand...

SUE

he plays guitar. he's very good...

JOHN

and this hurts and i'm standing there thinking,
"this doesn't need to be happening..." and i turn
on him. never spoke to him the whole time, just
turned on him and flipped him over onto the
ground and started pounding on his head. it's a
surface track so he's not getting too banged up but
i'm hitting him pretty good and sue's just standing
there...waiting.

SUE

i'd never seen this happen before...

JOHN

finally he stops squirming around and i hit him
one more time, you know high schoolers, right,

you go a bit overboard in a fight, and then i walk
over and grab her stuff and give it to her and we
take off. scirroco's still sitting there, people having
to jog around it, sun dancing off the hood of the
thing as we head home.

SUE

we walked all the way...

JOHN

noticed my reflection in it as we go by. bloody
nose, him grabbing at me...

SUE

...i had, like, two huge blisters the next day.

JOHN

and i kissed her, standing there on her porch, still
didn't say anything but we've been dating six years
since then and never heard back from the other
guy after that. (BEAT) i shot baskets with him
about a year ago, over at the elementary, and he
didn't seem so mad or nothing...

SUE

sometimes we fight, we do, like anybody else, or
break up...whatever. john dated someone for a
week or so, freshman year, i met this guy in a biol-
ogy class, john was on his mission. didn't last...
(BEAT) we're getting engaged this summer. we

already planned it...

JOHN

point being, it's our anniversary, right, and we're
hoping for this great time and whatnot, want it all
to be special. weekend in the city, girls wanna go
shopping in "the village" if there's time, whatever... (BEAT) we talked about taking the train on
the way back, alone. sleeping car...
pause.
...i'm kidding.

SUE

mid-terms last week everybody just needed to get
away.

JOHN

ends up we do go to my parent's house on sunday...dad makes me sit down, "you look like a
bushman," first thing out of his mouth—what's he
mean by that?—and he tries to give me a haircut!
halfway through my pre-med, he's still trying to
cut my bangs!

SUE

i thought it was kind of funny...i could hear them
arguing in the other room. his hair really does
look better when it's long. it does...

JOHN

but that's later. anyway...

SUE

so we make it to the city in, like, less than four
hours, weekend traffic, that's not bad.

JOHN

does it look stupid? seriously...no, i mean it. are
my ears funny at all?

SUE

$18.50 for ten hours parking, that's a lot, i
thought...and then we all walk over to the hotel,
the guys carrying these big dry cleaning bags over
their shoulders...

JOHN

we decided to go in on a room, all of us...not for
anything, i mean, you know...forget it. i'm just
telling you, so we could change and everything.
better than wrinkling our stuff up. right?

SUE

we get in, still a few hours before the party's going
to start, so we all decide to use the facilities, you
know, take a jacuzzi, whatever. lots of time to get
changed again...'s fun. (BEAT) i got back into my
dress...

JOHN

i'm tying up my shoes, lacing 'em up...she comes
out of the bathroom, like i said, this is six years
we've been going together and i'm still staring at
the best-looking girl i've ever seen. i'm just completely in love. serious...

SUE

makeup. try and put make up on in some hotel
bathroom and you'll understand the meaning of
devotion. sinks in those places, even the plaza, are
impossibly small, postage stamp of a mirror i'm
using...but i want to took nice for him. (BEAT) i
bought a new lipstick in the lobby. they had a
counter there...'s vivid. crimson...

JOHN

she steps into the living room of this hotel suite,
city full of models and actresses...the beautiful
people...and i can't see anything else. 's like we're
thrown back to the garden, the two of us, watching
one another across this great green meadow, my
side still hurting from the missing rib and all, but
she's revealed to me, golden hair and a face like
fresh snow and i'm thinking...hey, screw the bone,
you know, here's why he rested on the seventh
day. 'cause they can't get any better than this.
(BEAT) i mean, i'm not so poetic or whatever, but
this is exactly what i'm thinking.

SUE

the dress helps a lot, because i'm not going to kid
myself, it does, but i can see he's happy, and his
tux looks really handsome. it was going to be
great. a really good evening, i could feel it...

JOHN

and we walk downstairs, arm in arm. man, feels so
nice to stroll past all these people, i mean, rich
guys, girl like that on my arm! made me feel
strong, you know? powerful...the crowd almost
glides apart as we approach.

SUE

we've got nowhere to go. the party's not until later...

JOHN

'cause this bash is starting downtown, just kind of
picking up folks along the way, guys from home
are jumping in at any point and all set to meet at
the plaza...later.

SUE

nothing but possibilities...wherever we looked. i
really felt that, walking along.

JOHN

so on and on...couple hours pass, david's girlfriend, "karen," takes the lead at some point, walking us through the park...over by that one bridge,

the big pond? by the delacorte. moon's smiling
down and all, romance hanging over a night like
this out of some storybook, some tale by, maybe,
scott fitzgerald or those guys...i really do love this
girl. that's the thing that's screaming out in my
head right then...

SUE

he was holding my hand so tight...

JOHN

there's a swan or two out on the water. little
breeze, october, but still warm, you know how that
can be...perfect. a perfect night. and then, just off
to our left, there's this, like, patch of woods near
the path. comes this rustling...

SUE

i thought it might be some teenagers or who
knows what. we all started to walk a bit faster....

JOHN

i'm not scared but it's night, city all around...what
else can you do, girls with you? so we walk along.
(BEAT) and two guys, middle-aged guys, l.l. bean
shirts on and the whole thing...come out of the
dark. smiling. and i don't need a map to tell me
what's been going on...
pause
...i don't.

SUE

it was just two men. walking along...no big deal.

JOHN

coming out of the weeds, they were, off in the
park alone. and these smiles. i don't know, i just
don't know what to think about it. i mean, we're
going to this party, all dressed up, what should we
care, right? one dude looks like my father, a little,
it's dark but he had that look, right, that settled,
satisfied sort of...anyway, off they head, arms
linked together and nothing we say ever going to
change what they are...
pause.
dance all night, sue as stunning as she's ever
looked and i'm telling you, i can't get that picture,
the image of it, out of my head. those smiles. i can't
do it... (BEAT) but the party is great. it really is...

SUE

i haven't danced like that in a long time...

JOHN

it was, like, the beginning of a magical evening
...everything was right, it was pristine, you know?
soothing. and we just kept dancing, the two of us.
danced for hours...round and round.

SUE

they'd done the whole place, the room, i mean,

when we finally got inside...in blues, and golds, with these great moons, these golden crescents hanging above us...

JOHN

like smiles, like the moon smiling down...

SUE

i think we looked pretty nice together. looked like a couple, you know?

JOHN

it was fun, back like that, in the city...'s always fun. saw a lot of guys we know...

SUE

my little sister was there...there with some boy from greeley. he's in debate, he said. seemed nice enough...she likes him.

JOHN

we ran into sue's sister, did she mention that?

SUE

hadn't seen her since august...

JOHN

younger sister, maureen. with some kid...

SUE

he's not a member.

JOHN

ahh, he was okay. (BEAT) had a good band going.
reggae...

SUE

i'd never been to the plaza before, i mean, past it,
shopping and whatever, with my mom, but never
to it. it was tremendous! so much glass. high white
walls. it was like...a cake, some wedding cake, left
on the corner there. downtown. 's what it reminded me of... (BEAT) the whole thing, though...the
trip, dance and all...made me sleepy.

JOHN

sue went upstairs to our room, room we'd rented,
with karen and tim's girlfriend...patrice...

SUE

i'd known patrice since sunbeams...

JOHN

said they wanted to take a quick nap, just a half-
hour, whatever, then we'd go get a bite. this was,
like, maybe, one-thirty...

SUE

's a king-size bed. a gold comforter on it...

JOHN

so, we hung out downstairs a bit, talked to some
guys from home...david, tim, and me.

SUE

we all fell asleep, together on that bed...

JOHN

i was a touch bored. you know, room was warm,
and lots of people we didn't recognize...so i
suggested a walk. "let's head over to the park." about
six, seven guys all together. it was still nice out...

SUE

i'm not sure what time it was...

JOHN

we strolled around a bit, over by the paris theater,
some guy, younger guy, kicked over a garbage
can...i mean, it happens. you get together, doing
stuff, no big deal. 's just garbage...
pause.
fifteen, twenty minutes later we split up, lot of the
high schoolers want to get back to the bash, but us
three, tim, david, and me...no hurry. we just kind
'a wander around. hanging out. after a while, we
shoot over into central park, the 59th street
entrance...looking around, talking. 's really dark in
there. only lights coming from the buildings, way
off. kind of exciting...

SUE

i thought i looked up at two, or two-fifteen...but
i'm not sure. 'cause i kept sleeping...

JOHN

...and then i saw 'em. both of them. those guys...

SUE

i was so tired...

JOHN

they were saying "goodnight..." well, not saying it
exactly. but kissing. two men, grown men, standing in this park, public park in the middle of new
york and kissing like something out of a clark
gable film. tongues out, and the arms around each
other, and nothing else in the world matters to
these two...just finishing off the date, big night at
the symphony, or some foreign film, who knows?
but it's this "see you soon" and "thanks so much"
and hands all where they shouldn't be. i mean,
come on, i know the scriptures, know 'em pretty
well, and this is wrong. (BEAT) we all kind 'a
squeeze up against a couple trees, off in the shad-
ows, tim crouching on the ground, watching this.
out near "the ramble." oh man...man! you know,
you read about it, or even see that film, what is it,
with the "superman" guy? *deathtrap*, right, and
you live with it. don't love it, don't condone it for
the world, still. you go on living. live and let live,

whatever. but this, i figure, is flaunting it. i mean,
as much our park as theirs, and we're in town one
night, that's all, one...and we got 'a witness this?
pause.
men old enough to be our fathers—i mean,
middle-aged, and clutching at one another like
romeo and juliet! (BEAT) they whisper something,
and chuckle for a second, hand on each others
bottoms...i start to feel sick, i mean it, nauseous.
then a last peck on the cheek and one disappears
down a trail, headed for the west side. he's gone.
the other, one like my father, glances around,
taking in the night, i guess, big smile up at the
moon...and he kind of casually strolls over to this
"men's room." 50 yards off. concrete building,
with the steps down into it. whistling while he
goes...he was whistling. i don't even stop to think
this through, but motion the guys to follow me.

SUE

i thought about getting out of my dress, but i
couldn't move. all of us, we were sleeping so
peacefully... (BEAT) did you know patrice snores?
she does...a little.

JOHN

as we're moving down the landing into the
restroom, i glance at tim...'s got that look.
recognize that look anywhere. and he's starting
to smile...

SUE

i don't think i even dreamed that night...

JOHN

before going in i told the guys to hold off, wait out
here for me 'til they got my signal...and that's the
plan. wait for me to flush him out, make sure no
one wanders by. when i get inside, 's like another
world...walls are exploding with graffiti. place
stinks. two bulbs burnt out. some old dude curled
up, asleep in a corner. and our friend's legs, i spot,
patiently sitting in a stall. waiting, and not a care
in this world. i slip into the booth next to his, start
fumbling with my belt, this, that, and like clock-
work, this guy's hand comes up under my side of
the partition. his signal. pink fingers, wiggling up
at me. imploring. i notice this thin gold band on
his little finger, catching the light. (BEAT) so, i lay
my open palm in his and two minutes later we're
standing near the mirrors—big pieces of stainless
steel, really—standing, and sizing each other up.
small talk. name's "chet," he says, and i don't even
bat an eyelash as he moves in, his lips playing
across my cheek. let his tongue run along my teeth
and a hand, free hand, tracing down my fly...i just
smile at him, smile and even lick his chin for a
second, for a single second. i see his shoulders relax.
then i whistle. i let out a whistle that sends him
stumbling back, blinking, and kind of waving his
hands in the air as tim and dave appear in the

doorway. he looks at them, looks and comes back
from his fantasies long enough to touch down on
earth, a flicker in his eyes, realizing no good can
come from this...and starts babbling. this guy,
"chet," probably a vp some bank on park avenue,
and he's babbling and wetting himself like an
infant. i don't remember exactly, but i think he
even got on his knees, down on his knees and the
pleading. begging. (BEAT) my first shot catches
him against the cheek, just under the eye and he
slams into a sink. all snot and blood running
down. with so many of us hitting, tearing at him,
it's hard to get off a clean punch but i know i con-
nect a few more times. i feel his head, the back of
it, softening as we go, but i just find a new spot
and move on. tim kicking him long after he's
blacked out...

pause.

finally, we start to relax a bit, looking at what we've
done. exhausted. spent. i mean, this man is not
moving, may never move again and we know it's
time to leave. believe this, guy in the corner, sleeps
through it all?! (BEAT) before we go, tim leans
into it one more time, takes a little run at it,
smashing his foot against the bridge of this man's
nose and i see it give way. just pick up and move
to the other side of his face. wow. and then it's
silence. not a sound. and for the first time, we look
over at dave. tim and me. i mean, really look at
him. us together, tim, myself, that's one thing, it's

unspoken, our bond, but we don't know david.
don't really know him...what's he thinking? and
right then, as if to answer us through revelation
...he grabs up the nearest trash can, big wire mesh
thing, raises it above his head as he whispers,
"fag." i'll never forget that..."fag." that's all. and
brings that can down right on the spine of the guy,
who just sort of shudders a bit, expelling some air.
boom! right on his back, as i'm leaning down,
pulling that ring off his pinkie. (BEAT) i told you i
noticed it...

pause.

then, and i still can't even believe this, then tim
does the most amazing thing. this'll go down, the
record books. there, with the three of us over this
guy's body, he pulls out his key chain, opens the
little cylinder he's got dangling on the end of it,
and dumps the last of his oil, consecrated oil, on
this dude's forehead! i'm not kidding...dumps it
and starts offering up a short blessing. i mean, i'm
getting delirious, this is, like, almost surreal...and
halfway through, tim's praying along, we all start
giggling. like schoolboys, we're howling, tears running down, can't catch our breath we find it all so
funny! and that's how we leave him... (BEAT) slip
out, one by one, running back toward the plaza in
the dark and whooping it up like indians. war
cries, and running with just a trace of moonlight
dancing off the pond as we go...

SUE

the phone woke me up...

JOHN

we called the room from the street, wanted to take
the girls out to breakfast. say they'll be down in
fifteen minutes...
pause.
we waited outside.

SUE

i got the other girls up...took a minute, but i got
them up. i felt really refreshed...
pause.
...i did.

JOHN

dave's walking around on the curb, talking to himself, and tim pulls me aside. asks me, wants to
know one thing. "what?" i say. wants to know why
i touched the guy. let him kiss me. see, he'd seen it
happen. glanced inside, and seen it. (BEAT) but i
didn't know, didn't have an answer. isn't that
strange?

SUE

it was so quiet in the lobby as we were leaving. i
started tip-toeing out. isn't that funny?

JOHN

i couldn't answer him, and you know, he never
asked me again. he didn't. (BEAT) he pointed out
to me, though, that my shirt had blood on it, a
misting of blood, probably off the guy as i was getting the ring. my tux was covered, so, got 'a think
quick, i asked tim to hit me in the face, give me a
bloody nose so i could explain it to sue. (BEAT)
only hurt for a second...

SUE

we all met in front of the hotel, and i saw john's
face. aäah! all cut up like it was...see, he'd fallen
down, racing along the fountain out front, balanc-
ing on it, and slipped. scraped himself up and
blood on everything. (BEAT) silly games...

JOHN

had a great meal...you know, you can't get those
german sausages for breakfast, the big fat ones,
anywhere but manhattan. you can't...

SUE

i was eating my french toast, just eating along and
i notice this glint in my water glass. a spark of
light. (BEAT) john'd slipped a ring in it! a beautiful gold thing...i loved him so much at that
moment.

JOHN

"happy anniversary," i said...

SUE

it was a little big, but fit pretty well. had this wonderful leaf pattern, all the way around...

JOHN

looked nice on her. i liked it...

SUE

i kissed him there, in front of everybody, and he
blushed a bit. we all laughed. i can't tell you what a
wonderful weekend we had...

JOHN

we did end up taking the amtrak back up...just
sue and myself. dave dropped us at grand central
and, you know, lots of "thank you" and "see you
monday!" (BEAT) tim even gave me a hug. first
time he's even done that...

SUE

it was my idea...the train.

JOHN

and we saw our parents, stopped in sunday and
even made it to our meetings at the ward...that
was really nice.

SUE

i like relief society at home so much better...

JOHN

had dinner with the folks, then the late train up to boston.

SUE

you know, on the way back—it's funny, i shouldn't even bring this up—a fight broke out. well, not really a fight but this argument between a man and his girlfriend. a lot of yelling. she stands up, and starts pulling on her coat and this guy, i mean, middle of a crowded compartment, just backhands her. he did...

JOHN

knocked her up against the window. really hard...

SUE

everybody got quiet. i could feel john tense up, getting all tense, but the couple was, i don't know, kind of dirty-looking and they seemed like, you know, those kind of people—i don't know what i mean by that, exactly, but they were—so i asked john, whispered to him, to "let it go." (BEAT) and you know what? he didn't so much as bat an eye-lash. just kept holding my hand. holding it and playing with the ring on my finger. that made me so happy...

JOHN

i could see he'd given her a bloody nose...

SUE

and they pretty much quieted down right after
that. 's no big deal...

JOHN

anyway...

SUE

anyway, we are getting engaged this summer. for
sure. did i tell you that?

JOHN

and finally, as we tumbled along toward massachusetts, nearly midnight...i could feel sue fall asleep
against my shoulder. all warm. protected.

SUE

i hope it's a fall wedding, you know? i always think
they're the most beautiful...

JOHN

but not me...i couldn't drift off. just couldn't do it.
so i sat up, watching the lights dance by, the moon
grinning down. and you know, i started whistling
to myself. i did...

SUE

i was sleeping. asleep there on john's arm, but i'd swear i could hear music...

JOHN

not loud, i mean, don't even recall the tune. but i was whistling, i was. that much i remember...

SUE

...this beautiful music as i was sleeping. like the sound of angels calling us home...

they sit together in silence for a moment. finally, they rise and embrace, waiting for their picture to be taken. they smile broadly.

harsh blast of a camera's flashbulb.

silence. darkness.

medea redux

silence. darkness.

**woman sits alone in a chair
at an institutional-style
table. a harsh light hangs
down directly overhead.
a tape player, water carafe
and cup, cigarettes, and an
ashtray are close at hand.**

**woman finishes a cigarette,
stubs it out, and slowly
begins to speak.**

WOMAN

...can i just speak? 's that okay? i mean, i'll talk
about, but...i got 'a sort of ease into it, you know?
'cause i was never, like, this major talker or anything...like to keep things to myself. some people'd
call it "private" or whatever, but it's more like just
being sort 'a "inward." right? i'm an inward kind 'a
person...i think it depends a lot on the way you
grow up, you know, family and all, and i just
ended up more inward than anything...anyway, i
found that a lot of times, when you ask for stuff,
or, like, have maybe questions to things...there's
not always an answer out there. you can ask over
and over, but you don't all the time hear something back... (BEAT) speaking 'a that, you can
hear me, okay, right? can ya? i guess so...

**she begins to speak, then
stops, considers. finally,
she begins again, very
slowly.**

...it's interesting, you know, how things'll work
out. well, not "out," i guess, not so much that as
maybe just "through." right? things get worked
through...or work themselves through. we
probably don't have all that much to do with
it. we like to think we do, though, right? god, like
we're in on all the big planetary decisions and shit,
you know? but, uh-uh...you wanna know what i
feel, i think we're just spinning around out here,
completely out 'a whack and no way of ever getting it right again, i mean, back on track or whatever...just can't do it. see, we been doing things
wrong for so long now that it all starts to feel okay
after a while, you know, like this is how it oughta
be. (BEAT) there's a greek word for that...i
learned it in school. he taught it to me...well, i
guess i more like "heard" it from him, if i'd 'a
learned it i could tell you what it is, right? yeah. i
know it's greek, though, i caught that much, but i
don't remember what it was...

**she thinks quietly for a
moment.**

no...'s too long ago now. had something to do with
the world, the whole thing, coming off its axis or

something, going off in the wrong direction from
how it's all supposed to be. and its the fault of
people. or "mortals," that's what my teacher said,
"mortals are to blame." see, he said it was simply
the fact that—and i never could understand this,
maybe i just didn't listen good enough, that was
the usual problem—but he said it all stemmed
from just our being mortal. right? (BEAT) so,
then every problem we got is from being mortals
...or humans, that's what "mortals" means...and
just because we are what we are, these "mortals,"
it's, like, our fault. explain me that...

**she stops for a moment and
lights a cigarette.**

you know, a lot of times i just couldn't make clear
what was coming out 'a his mouth. he was really
smart, though, had, like, two college degrees or
something, and still wanted to work at public
school. i kind 'a admired that. i was in his class,
one of 'em, his first year. 's great...he took us, my
class anyway, on a bunch 'a stuff, field trips, like
museums, and up to chicago one time. that was
fun. we went there, maybe twenty-five or so of us,
the school bus, and i remember we were going
along that one road, runs past the lake up there...
god, that was beautiful! he looked back, my
teacher did, sitting up by the driver, and saw all of
us kids smashed up against our windows and
staring out, every one of us with our eyes glued to

that water! so, he had the driver pull off at an exit
and we got, maybe, fifteen minutes or so to run
around on the beach...this was november...chase
each other, throw rocks, whatever, but all i did was
stand there, stand down by the edge of the surf
and watch the waves coming in. there in my little
red windbreaker. and i dunno, i felt like an astro-
naut. or a kind 'a time explorer, maybe, some
scout or something, sent on ahead, down to earth
to see just what the fuck all the fuss's about...and
taking it all in for the first time. you know? i still
remember that. 's kind 'a like that moment in that
one movie, with all the monkeys and that one guy,
he does those commercials for...*planet of the apes*,
that's the one. it's like that, remember, when he
rides down the beach and realizes that he's home
after all, and there's no going back, and he's
screaming and everything, pounding his fist up at
the sky, but he's still sort 'a caught up in it all, too,
like, taken in by the awesomeness of what he's
seen...i mean, it was better than that, i thought,
maybe just because of my age at the time, it was
better, but it reminded me of that a little. it did...

> **she stops, taking an extra
> long drag on her smoke.**

you know what's funny? he hit on me, my teacher
did, on one of those trips. yeah. not on that one,
this was at the maritime center a couple months
later...scared the shit out 'a me! i didn't even

know what he was doing at first—i mean, okay, i
did, but i was, like, thirteen—and that's just not
what you're expecting at that age. well, maybe it
never is...he came up behind me at the observation tank, right, where they've got the sharks and
everything. see, this other teacher was with us and
she wanted to take the rest of the children on
down the passageway—'cause they have a place
where you can handle different sea things, shells
and crabs and stuff, and the shark tank has this
dark room connected to it so that you can stand
there and see without a glare all over the windows,
and some kids were sort 'a scared—but i was
always interested in sharks and all that, i was. you
know, you have to pick a vocation in seventh
grade, they make you do that in junior high, on
this "career day," right? and i chose "marine biolo-
gist." i did. out 'a all the other kinds of things they
had there, i picked that one, 'cause i love the water,
always have...so, my teacher said it'd be okay if i
stayed and watched, we'd catch up later... (BEAT)
well, i'm keeping my eye on this one big hammerhead, that's a species of shark—you probably knew
that—and he's darting in real close to the glass, this
hammerhead is...suddenly, i feel all this weight up
against me. my teacher is pushing me forward with
his body, up onto the observation windows, and i
can't move. he never said anything while it was
happening, i mean, to me—i could hear him whis-
pering something about the "tragic nobility of sea

creatures," some shit like that—and all i can see, i
can't turn at all, the way he's got me held there, all
i can see is this shark, the one i'd been watching,
coming out of the murk and sweeping past me,
again and again...and it's not 'till he's right on top
of me, and turned each time, that i can see his eye.
he turns past the glass at the last second and his
eye just sort 'a rolls back all white as he passes
...fuck, that was scary. i've never forgotten it. that
feeling. his weight on me, and watching as that
hammerhead just kept circling around... (BEAT)
well, what the hell, it's easy to scare a kid. right?

**she plays a moment with the
butt of her cigarette in
the ashtray.**

anyway, he wouldn't look at me after that, my
teacher, not even a glance, the whole rest of the
trip. and he was always real nice before, and funny
to me...i mean, not in a bad way, not like inappro-
priately so, i don't think, but—no, i wasn't even a
"teacher's pet" or whatever—he was just sort 'a
open with me. jokes, and showing me pictures in
magazines, like, after that career thing he would
hang up undersea stuff in class, and bringing in
pieces 'a coral to look at...we were starting to be
friends, i thought. at least sort of friendly. because
it's hard, i think, for a teacher in school, like,
junior high, where nobody cares, kids just wanna
do sports, and dances, hang out with their friends,
you know...so, if you meet a person who is actually

interested, like i was, and i really was—i wasn't the
smartest or remembered the most, like i said,
but—i was genuinely interested in things. i wanted
to learn, right, i felt like i needed to comprehend a
little about the universe, you know? i did. 'cause it
intrigues me. the way it works. yeah. (BEAT) and i
think a teacher can pick up on that. and he just
responded to it...so, we started to sort 'a hang out
a bit...just at school. the library, or looking at slides
in the resource center. lunchtimes. (BEAT) it was
good, umm...'s good, that's all. i mean, fuck, i was
thirteen, okay, it was nice to have somebody look
at you and not say to pick up your socks...some-
thing like that. let's face it, thirteen's a pretty shitty
age, right?
pause.
but he wouldn't look over at me after that...

she stops a moment.

he did give me a ride home, though. from school.
he did do that. i mean, nothing, not a look on the
outing, sits way away from me on the bus, but
back at our building, see, he's responsible for us,
and all the parents are there, this is a friday, and
my dad doesn't show. he doesn't show up. we go
into the office, call his work, nothing at home,
and he doesn't come. half-hour goes by, nobody at
school but us. sitting there on the curb, waiting for
my dad. finally he says, my teacher, he can drop
me if i want. he drove this late model peugeot—i

remember 'cause i once asked him to teach me
how to say it—kind of a cream color peugeot, and
he said he'd run me home if i'd like that. 's what
he said, "if you'd like that." (BEAT) in the car, like
this was yesterday, i recall he had this woman
singing on the tape player, real soft and painful, i
remember, 'cause i had to ask who this was. i
mean, this was not the bee gees and i'd never
heard anything like it. so fragile-sounding, you
know? he said it was "billie holiday," that was her
name, and it was all he ever played. first thing
he'd said to me, i mean, practically, in five hours is
"billie holiday." and he smiled. it was dark out, but
i could see him smiling there, we're sitting at a
light, and he says, "she's all i ever listen to." and
then, "you kind of remind me of her, you know?
you always seem just a little bit sad. smiling, but
sad. i like that..." (BEAT) the fuck did that mean?
you know? because, listen, you don't say stuff like
that to a thirteen-year-old, okay? you just don't,
uh-uh, 'cause she'll be yours for life. i mean it. if
you do, she will be...
pause.
not in front of my house, but down from it, a
block maybe, he pulls over, there's a florist shop
and its closed, this time of the evening, and he
parks in the little lot they have there...he kissed
me. jesus, he kissed me like, i guess, you imagine
how it must've been when they first invented it,
like back in the days of myths and shit, when, you

know, men were heroes and you could get kissed
like that and you'd wait a lifetime for him to
return, you would, and you could still taste him on
your lips, years later. because back then kisses still
meant something. that's what he kissed me like...

**she takes a sip of water.
she fiddles again with the
edge of the water cup but
doesn't drink.**

i really don't wanna, umm, elaborate too much on,
well, you know, cover all the relationship stuff a
whole lot, 'cause if you've talked to him you know
it already, anyway, right? maybe more than you
want to... (BEAT) we started seeing each other,
you know, as much as a junior high school teacher
and a thirteen-year-old can see each other. that's
what we began to do. we started doing that. and i
know what you're thinking, or have thought it to
each other, laughing and stuff, that it's my own
fault or that he was some type 'a molester, whatever, but you wouldn't really be true about that.
either side of that. we, umm...just liked each other.
and would kiss and things. not so much, but kiss
and little hugs and stuff—i'd sneak into his class-
room at lunch for, like, just seconds sometimes,
and we'd hug—that's what we'd do.
pause.
my fourteenth birthday...'s in march, i'm a
pisces..."the fish." how 'bout that? i guess it was

really the weekend of, the actual day fell on a
thursday, but that saturday, he, umm, picked me
up at the library, the downtown branch, where i
did book sorting on a volunteer basis, 'cause you
get a bunch of privileges and stuff if you do it
twice a month...but i told her, the volunteer coor-
dinator, she was just a high school girl anyway, i
told her i felt sick that day and he picked me up
and we went driving. i asked where but he said,
"it's a surprise," so i sat back in the ol' peugeot,
the sun roof was up, 's a real nice day out, and just
kind 'a drifted off to the sound of the wind rushing by. the wind and billie holiday singing sad on
the back speakers...

> **she stops, gathering her
> thoughts a moment.**

when we got to chicago, he drove straight to the
lake, to this pier where he'd rented a boat for us,
beautiful red speedboat, and god, it was so exciting for me! he just kept doing things like this, and
there's a picnic basket and it was great, just great
...to be out there, in the water, on this boat with
him, it was just real lovely... (BEAT) he gave me a
bracelet, it was all wrapped up, in wax paper,
inside my sandwich! yeah, you believe that, he'd
hollowed out my bread and put my present inside
there, and i loved that, that was just cute...and i
got, ahh, this beautiful, like, picture book of several
greek stories, mostly of euripides, 'cause, see, he

felt euripides was the most, what, "humanistic"...
had, like, the most humanity of the greek writers.
he said he was the one most at war with this...
(BEAT) shit, still can't think of that word, but he
was the guy who was really angry about the world
being all fucked up just because we happened to
be mortals...anyhow, it had a bunch 'a nice draw-
ings and he said i'd like it even more as i got
older... (BEAT) i still have it.
silence.
i, umm...found out about the baby, that i was
going to have one, in late april, the 23rd, i guess,
and i didn't cry. i should've, fucking kid myself,
you know, but sometimes you can go along, years
even, and not feel like you're growing up at all,
and then there's times when you age a ton, like, in
a couple 'a seconds. you know? so, i found out and
went straight to his place, i mean, called first, but
went there and we discussed it all. talked a long
time... (BEAT) we talked, like i said, and, you know,
he seemed, and this caught me, 'cause i didn't
know what he'd think, but he was all excited! not
yelling, or all adult and shit, and said he loved
children, could think of nothing better than having
a son or something. said we'd have to be careful—
i mean, we both understood the situation—but i
promised him i wouldn't tell anybody who the
father was, no matter if my dad got really shitty
about it—and he did, believe me—or school, or
whatever. i said i'd keep our secret...we made a

pledge together, there on his sofa, and i kept it.
(BEAT) he told me that day, he said he had to go
away for a couple weeks, just the end of summer,
he was finishing up another of his degrees at del-
phi, that's a university, and then we'd, you know,
make some plans. (BEAT) that was hard, 'cause i
was scared, i'm not gonna pretend i wasn't, but
getting his degree was a big thing, and could help
us, too, he said...and so we talked for awhile, and
we kissed. god, you know for being this big guy, he
was really gentle to me...and then i went home. i
went to my house with our baby inside me, and
watched *hogan's heroes* on tv, like i did every afternoon. i mean, what else are you gonna do, right?
(BEAT) i just need a little water...

**she pours a touch more into
her cup and sips.**

okay. umm, what else? ahh...when i found out he'd
left his position at school—this was by a fluke, anyway, i was at the general office during the summer,
which was not that far from our house, bringing
them a vaccination report on my brother, and the
lady there, the secretary, said, "oh, i heard about
your arts and sciences teacher at gardner," my
school, "we're sure sorry to lose him, aren't we?"—
i didn't hear much else, really, just that she said,
"well, i suppose they need good teachers in
phoenix as much as they do anywhere..." (BEAT)
but i didn't ask for an address or anything, i didn't,

because i was standing there, in that office, suddenly standing there, fourteen years old with a
baby in me and this woman yacking on about my
brother needing a german measles booster, and
did i know if he'd had one yet, and i was frozen in
time. 's like the heavens had opened above me, at
that very second, and all i could hear was the universe. this woman in front of me talking on like i
was her godchild and all i could make out was the
howl of the cosmos...and you know what? it was
laughing. it was. all it's attention was suddenly
turned and it was laughing, laughing down at
me...

**she stops and slowly lights
another cigarette.**

like i said, there's a bunch 'a shit you don't need to
hear twice, and i don't want your sympathy, okay, i
don't, so we'll skip the hardship stuff about when i
did tell my family, and being pulled out 'a school,
the move to my aunt's house...sound familiar? i
told you before, or if i didn't, i meant to...this
story's nothing special, really, practically the only
part that's of any interest is that it happened to
me...you know? (BEAT) anyways, billie, that's my
son, billie, "william," whatever...was born. a beautiful
boy. just quite great, and although every mom
goes off on that, he was. i mean it. he's great, and,
umm, without getting all shitty about it, i give
birth and a bunch 'a years pass. okay? i did finally

make contact with his father, sent a couple letters, and he wrote me back right away, this was, ohh, maybe a year, eighteen months later...just long enough to make him wonder, you know? i was still only about sixteen at the time, so i guess he was pretty scared about the whole thing—'s what he said on paper, anyway—and asked if i could understand. not forgive...understand. (BEAT) i, ahh, let him know that our pact was still safe, and this wasn't, like, some money thing, i just wanted him to have, if he wouldn't mind so much, a sort 'a relationship with billie, through the mail or whatever. i knew there was nothing for us, well, you know, not after that...but i'd send pictures and stuff, we ended up doing it through a postal box, and he got to know his son that way. that's how it happened. a few presents now and again, and he had a son, and the son's mother loved him, and kept the secret all while the father was away. and i know you'll think i'm just talking shit now, but honestly, if i closed my eyes and thought about it, i could still feel his kiss on my lips. even then...
long pause.
the rest you know...on his fourteenth birthday, billie and me, we rented a car—we were living in utah by then, out with some mormon relatives at that point—and we drove to arizona to meet his father. we'd planned this, the two of us, by letter, and agreed it'd be just the one time...he was, umm, you know, married by this time, married

and teaching in phoenix. no children, though,
isn't that funny? no kids 'cause his wife had a part
of her uterus, i guess, some thing, that wouldn't
work properly. but they didn't adopt and just kept
trying naturally. over and over. i thought that was
the only real sad part 'a all this—so, it'd just be
this once, at a motel that he'd picked in town. one
time when we'd all sit down and see each other.
again. at least, the two of us, again...

> **she fiddles with the
> edge of the tape player.**

this thing's almost run out...

> **she looks up but there is
> no answer.**

okay. (BEAT) we met at the room. 's a terribly hot
day, at least for december it was, 's how i remember it, anyway, and we were tired from the travel,
but he was there, as promised. hardly seemed any
older, which kind 'a sucked, i thought, 'cause i'd
changed—i mean, look at me, right?—and it was
this big moment for billie, 's all excited, and we
even hugged, and it was in that second, as he
leaned in to kiss my cheek, his head turned
toward me and maybe it was just the light, the sun
coming in the room, but i saw something there,
there in his eyes...he loved this boy, all that shit
he'd said to me years ago, it was true about kids.

he loved 'em. but also...he was satisfied. i could see
that, satisfaction on his face...because he'd gotten
away with it all. that's what i saw, shining in his
eyes, as he moved forward to kiss me. he'd beaten
fate...and gotten away with it. (BEAT) after dinner,
we had a bucket of store-bought chicken in the
room, billie got a couple packages—one was a
book of myths, imagine that—he said he wanted to
see us again before we left. he had to run to school
for about an hour, a science fair, i guess, but he'd
be back. he promised he'd be right back. the last
time i saw him, there at the door, he mentioned
that word, that...umm, well, whatever, he said it
and smiled, as he stepped out onto the balcony
he smiled to me and whispered, "maybe it's not
our fault after all. i mean, we're just human,
right?"
pause.
billie was already in the bathroom, we'd driven
straight through, and i could hear the water running. he was in his bath. god, he loved the tub!
since he was tiny, he loved it. so, i knew he was in
there, the water filling up around him, and "lady
day"—'s what he liked to call billie holiday, 's her
nickname, and he called her that—playing on his
tape player. "stormy weather." i, ahh, went into the
room, the bathroom, and i could see him there,
through a little opening in the liner he had pulled
shut, eyes closed and the steam coming up. he
didn't really struggle, couldn't actually, the shock

of it, i suppose, when the recorder first hit the
water...there was really only a quick kind 'a snap-
ping sound, like the pop of a flashbulb or whatnot,
and then the softer sound of him, billie, as he
kicked a second or two in the water. i turned the
taps off a little later... (BEAT) after, i just sat there,
on the linoleum, and watched him, lying in that
cloudy pool of bath water. his eyes open and so
still. i thought i could almost see, i mean, if i
squinted, i could almost make out..."adakia," that's
the word. the word i was trying, you know, that's
it. "the world out of balance." you can look it up if
you wanna, but i'm sure that's the one...i knew it'd
come to me, if i waited long enough.

> **she lights another smoke.**

i was picked up in vegas, at a restaurant, you're
aware of that, though, obviously...and brought
back here. and that's it. so, now you know. i mean,
what you really wanted, anyway, right? now you
know...yes. i planned it, yes. but...maybe longer
than you thought, huh? lots longer...

> **she laughs to herself.**

and i worry about what's gonna happen, i mean,
to me and all, i do—'s natural, though, right, to
wonder about things—but i'll tell you. tell you
what gets me through today, the next hour...it's
him.

pause.

i can almost see 'em, you know, i can, down there in phoenix, probably wandering around on some playground at school, a saturday, and he's just stumbling there by himself near the monkey bars. can't be consoled, right, the truth all spilled out now like it is, and all these tears running down, yelling up at the sky, these torrents of tears and screaming, the top of his lungs, calling up into the universe, "why?! why?!!" over and over. (BEAT) but you know what? in my fantasy, there's never an answer. uh-uh. there never is...

she sits and smokes now as the tape player continues to quietly hum on.

silence. darkness.